RABBITS EAT POOP!

By Roberto Betances

Gareth Stevens
PUBLISHING

Please visit our website, www.garethstevens.com. For a free color catalog of all our high-quality books, call toll free 1-800-542-2595 or fax 1-877-542-2596.

Cataloging-in-Publication Data

Names: Betances, Roberto.
Title: Rabbits eat poop! / Roberto Betances.
Description: New York : Gareth Stevens Publishing, 2018. | Series: Nature's grossest | Includes index.
Identifiers: ISBN 9781538209493 (pbk.) | ISBN 9781538209516 (library bound) | ISBN 9781538209509 (6 pack)
Subjects: LCSH: Rabbits–Juvenile literature. | Rabbits–Behavior–Juvenile literature.
Classification: LCC QL737.L32 B48 2018 | DDC 599.32–dc23

Published in 2018 by
Gareth Stevens Publishing
111 East 14th Street, Suite 349
New York, NY 10003

Copyright © 2018 Gareth Stevens Publishing

Designer: Laura Bowen
Editor: Therese Shea

Photo credits: Cover, p. 1 Vicki Jauron, Babylon and Beyond Photography/Moment Open/ Getty Images; pp. 3–24 (background) Oleksii Natykach/Shutterstock.com; p. 5 SolStock/E+/ Getty Images; p. 7 Ng Yin Jian/Shutterstock.com; p. 9 Geza Farkas/Shutterstock.com; p. 11 JSR.Photography/Shutterstock.com; p. 13 MG Photos/Shutterstock.com; p. 15 emka74/ Shutterstock,com; p. 17 (main) Roine Magnusson/The Image Bank/Getty Images; p. 17 (inset) Fiver, der Hellseher/Wikimedia Commons; p. 19 T. M. McCarthy/Shutterstock.com; p. 21 Pressmaster/Shutterstock.com.

Printed in China

CPSIA compliance information: Batch #CW18GS: For further information contact Gareth Stevens, New York, New York at 1-800-542-2595.

CONTENTS

Boldface words appear in the glossary.

They Eat *What*?

Rabbits are some of the cutest animals. Nearly everyone loves petting a rabbit's soft fur. But these lovable creatures have some gross **behaviors**, too. They eat their own poop! And it's healthy for them!

A Bit About Bunnies

There are 28 species, or kinds, of rabbits. They're many colors and sizes. All have long ears and a short tail. Many rabbit species dig **burrows** under the ground. They may live in groups called colonies.

Rabbits' eyes are on the sides of their head. They can see behind them without turning around! Rabbits have long, powerful back legs, too. They can jump great **distances**. Some can hop more than 9 feet (2.7 m) at once!

Plenty of Plants

Rabbits only eat plants. During warm months, they eat **herbs**, peas, grasses, and any other green plants they can find. In the winter, it's hard for rabbits to find green plants. They eat small branches, bark, and buds instead.

Rabbits need to eat a lot of plants so that their body gets enough **nutrients** to stay healthy. However, plants are hard for rabbits to fully **digest**. That's why rabbits make two kinds of poop!

To Eat or Not to Eat

Rabbits have a special **digestive system**. It forms two kinds of droppings. One kind is dry and round. This is solid waste called feces (FEE-seez). It contains matter that the body can't use or needs to get rid of.

15

The other kind of rabbit dropping is made in a different part of its digestive system. It's sometimes called a night dropping, but can happen anytime. It contains many **vitamins**. It's soft, dark, and bunched together, like grapes. When rabbits pass this, they eat it right away.

Once eaten, this special poop goes to another part of the rabbit's stomach. There, the body takes out the remaining nutrients. Whatever is left passes out of the rabbit's body as feces. It won't be eaten again.

18

19

Gross, but Good!

Rabbits that don't eat the "good poop" get very sick. They may even die! This behavior is important to keep rabbits alive. Can you think of gross behaviors people have that are good for them, too?

GLOSSARY

behavior: the way an animal acts, or behaves

burrow: a hole or tunnel in the ground that an animal makes to live in or for safety

digest: to change food that has been eaten into simpler forms that can be used by the body

digestive system: the body parts that work together to turn food into forms that the body can use

distance: the amount of space between two places or things

herb: a plant or part of a plant sometimes used to give taste to food

nutrient: something that plants, animals, and people need to live and grow

vitamin: a natural matter that is often found in foods and helps a body be healthy

FOR MORE INFORMATION

BOOKS

Foran, Jill. *Rabbit.* New York, NY: AV2 by Weigl, 2013.

Glover, David, and Penny Glover. *Rabbit.* Mankato, MN: Sea-to-Sea Publications, 2008.

Heneghan, Judith. *Love Your Rabbit.* New York, NY: Windmill Books, 2013.

WEBSITES

Eastern Cottontail Rabbit
animals.nationalgeographic.com/animals/mammals/cottontail-rabbit/
Read about this common rabbit species.

Rabbits: Habits, Diet & Other Facts
www.livescience.com/28162-rabbits.html
Check out many more facts about rabbits.

INDEX